SETTLE & CARLISLE
SUNSET

Edited by Michael Harris

Contents

Published by

IAN ALLAN LTD

Terminal House Shepperton TW17 8AS
Telephone: Walton-on-Thames (0932) 228950
Fax: 0932 232366   Telex: 929806 IALLAN G
Registered Office: Terminal House Shepperton TW17 8AS
Phototypeset and Printed by Ian Allan Printing at their works at
Coombelands in Runnymede, England

Introduction

AT THE time of writing (late October 1988), it seems impossible to guess what will happen to the Settle & Carlisle line. The Government's dual-track approach of waiting to allow new evidence to be heard for retention of train services, at the same time inviting private buyers to bid for the line seems more political game-playing than a genuine response to resolve the future for one of Britain's greatest civil engineering achievements.

In more enlightened times, initiatives to evolve a joint enterprise by public and private interests to make the most of a magnificent legacy and national asset would surely have been encouraged. This option appears to have been ruled out. It is likely to be so because of Government views that privatisation of public assets represents the panacea for all ills. This recipe seems destined in time to apply to all British Rail's operations: in which form is not yet clear.

For its part, British Rail has made it known that it sees no future on its own account for the Settle & Carlisle which is understandable — at first sight — if it is to realise Government targets to reduce its reliance on public funds. BR's Provincial Sector has said that if it is required to maintain passenger services over the S&C it will, otherwise it would like to be relieved of its responsibility. Others — notably the Friends of the Settle-Carlisle Line Association — believe that BR is missing the point. Imaginatively run, the S&C could further improve on what many believe is its present ability to be one of the better revenue generators of the Provincial publicly funded Sector. That evidence is presented as part of this book. One hopes that it will prove — even at this late hour — to convince those who will make the final decision on the S&C's future.

But of course the S&C is more than a prosaic pawn in the arena of public decision making. It is a living expression of our architectural and engineering heritage. It is a notable monument to the business enterprise of a form of transport that created modern Britain and contributed greatly to our culture and standard of life. Its ability to convey large numbers of people through some of Britain's grandest, most striking and most beautiful countryside contributes to that standard of life; not only that, but it gives access to that countryside for recreation and enjoyment. The revival of steam working over the S&C contributes yet more pleasure, not only as a spectacle but as an opportunity for railwaymen to give of their best. And they have.

All this is at risk — and it should not be so. There is still time for that new initiative to make a real future for the Settle & Carlisle. In the meantime, this short appreciation of the line is presented as a contribution to the debate and, one hopes, as enjoyable reading. Some of the spirit and atmosphere of the line as it *is* and as it *was* comes through in its contents, not least the late Derek Cross's portrait of a stretch of railway that is almost without equal for devotees. We hope you will enjoy it!

Michael Harris
Editor

Cover:
LMS '5' 4-6-0 No 5305 crosses Ais Gill Viaduct with the 'Thames-Eden Express' of 10 May 1986. The '5' worked from Carlisle-York.
W. A. Sharman

Title page:
Memories of regular steam working — 'Jubilee' 4-6-0 No 45562 *Alberta* begins the climb from Stainforth, north of Settle, with the Saturday 06.40 Birmingham-Leeds-Glasgow on 5 August 1967. *Paul Claxton*

Contents page:
The grand scenery at Batty Moss, with the usual accompaniment of cloud and sunlight — on the days of better weather! A Class 50 approaches Ribblehead Viaduct with a diverted Sunday morning Manchester Victoria-Glasgow Central express on 10 September 1972.
J. H. Cooper-Smith

Back cover colour
Duchess of Hamilton at Ribblehead with a down 'Cumbrian Mountain Express' on 20 February 1982. *J. H. Cooper-Smith*

Bottom:
'Jubilee' No 5593 *Kolhapur* silhouetted as it crosses Lunds Viaduct, north of Garsdale, with a Leeds-Carlisle 'Cumbrian Mountain Express' on 21 March 1987. *W. A. Sharman*

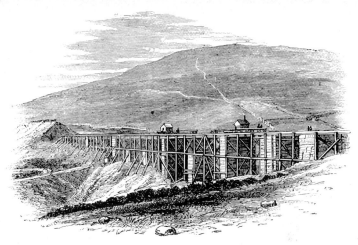

ARTEN GILL VIADUCT IN COURSE OF CONSTRUCTION.

The S&C
searching for a suitor

Chris Leigh

LIKE a beautiful but ageing woman wanting a husband, the Settle and Carlisle line is being offered, complete with a 'dowry', to anyone who will take it on and operate it as a private enterprise tourist attraction. David Mitchell, then Minister for Public Transport, announced the controversial decision to the House of Commons on 16 May 1988 and on the following afternoon held a press briefing. Just four journalists attended that meeting. I was one of them, and wrote this immediately afterwards.

Left:
Armathwaite Viaduct on a glorious late Spring day — LMS '5' No 5407 and 'Jubilee' No 5690 *Leander* **make a fine sight at the head of the Carlisle-bound 'Cumbrian Mountain Express' of 29 May 1982.** *W. A. Sharman*

Below:
The 10.40 Carlisle-Leeds of 10 May 1986 passes the site of the Garsdale water troughs, renowned as the highest located in the world. Motive power is Class 47/4 No 47449. *W. A. Sharman*

The salient points from the 16 May announcement were:
1 That the Minister is 'minded' to consent to BR's closure proposal for the S&C and the Blackburn-Hellifield line.
2 That the final decision would be delayed until 30 November 1988 in order to consider *any* further developments and to allow time for any prospective private operator to put forward its proposals.
3 After 30 November, BR would be required to operate the line for a further four months before either closure or handing over to a successor.
4 BR would be prepared to negotiate a 'dowry' with a suitable private sector operator. This would be likely to include the track, structures, signalling and land. In addition, BR would undertake to remove and pay for lengths of continuously welded rail if these were not required by the operator. This could provide up to £850,000 of working capital for the new owner to commence operations.

Reaction to the announcement was swift and to the point. In a news release the Friends of the Settle & Carlisle Line Association said they were 'shocked and baffled' . . . and described it as a 'slap in the face.' The Chairman of West Yorkshire PTA called it 'devastating news'. These organisations feel that it is essential for the line to remain part of the BR network.

When speaking to journalists, David Mitchell referred to the significance of the S&C as the last main line 'built with pick and shovel', and to its scenic attractions and outstanding civil engineering features. However, BR had quoted current annual losses of £1 million on a £2 million turnover and, even with modernisation, it was felt that this figure could not be reduced below £850,000. In addition, BR wished to be rid of the problem of repairing Ribblehead Viaduct, although there are considerable differences of opinion over the likely cost of repairs. BR repaired one arch during the summer of 1988 in order to accurately assess the work involved.

Above:
Dent station on 11 August 1983, with the green painted Class 40 No 40122/D200 on the 16.00 Leeds-Carlisle. *C. Addis*

Above right:
A Glasgow-Nottingham express at Ais Gill, overlooked by Wild Boar Fell. An October 1981 picture. *J. H. Cooper-Smith*

Among the offers of support for any private rescue bid have been financial and practical help from construction and renovation firms as well as potential sponsorship from the hotel and catering industry. English Heritage is offering £1 million towards viaduct repairs. In contrast, the Minister felt that the offer of £500,000 from local authorities was not as helpful as it seemed. This would comprise three annual payments of £166,000 and nothing further. The offer was made on condition that BR continued to maintain and operate the line, that the line's future would be guaranteed for at least 20 years, and that no further requests for financial support would be made. The current level of revenue support at £70,000 per annum would not be renewed when it expires in two years' time. It was subsequently suggested to the writer by a local authority journalist that the people involved in the hard-fought battle to obtain any support from some local authorities would be somewhat 'miffed' at the attitude to their offer.

On the practical side, it has not been really clear just how much of the S&C route is on offer. Clearly, any private operator would find it essential to have physical connections into the BR network at Carlisle and either Skipton or Leeds. This would be a matter for negotiation but it was suggested that matters would be easier at the Carlisle end than at the southern end of the line. In any event, it would seem that the private operator would require running rights over BR track. If, as seems likely, the operator were to opt for diesel or DMU operation then the question of privately-owned preserved diesels running over BR would arise. If steam traction were to be used, BR would be unlikely to relish regular and frequent steam movements 'under the wires' at Carlisle or Leeds because of the corrosive action of steam exhaust on catenary.

I questioned the Minister at the 16 May briefing as to whether the private company was likely to be simply the 'custodian' of the line's fixed assets, leasing running rights to BR or other operators. In answer, it was envisaged that it would be a full-fledged preserved railway operation. References were made to the Mid-Hants Railway, with regard to shared interchange facilities with BR, and also to the Severn Valley which the Minister pointed out had an annual turnover similar to that required to operate the S&C.

Taking the point further, I raised the question of operating the S&C under light railway regulations — hardly an attractive prospect, with 25mph speed restrictions etc. Here, a DoT official indicated that there were several options which might be considered. It was accepted that the Light Railway Order system might not be attractive. An alternative might be for BR to form the S&C into a subsidiary company which would then handover its assets and liabilities, together with its main line status, to the new operator. Another possibility would be through Parliamentary powers.

Clearly, the Minister and the DoT felt that there were good prospects for finding a suitable private operator. One wonders whether the whole package has been put together because such a suitor is already

showing interest, although this is denied. Railway preservation schemes have been notoriously slow to get off the ground, and if a genuine preserved railway operation is envisaged then the few months allowed scarcely gives it much chance. After all, the timescale of the announcement would see the complete closure of the line on 1 April 1989.

From the practical viewpoint only the largest of preserved railways comes anywhere near generating the income and enthusiast support which would be required. The S&C is three times the length of the longest of these. Instead of the vast West Midlands conurbation from which to draw support (as in the case of the Severn Valley Railway), the S&C boasts surroundings of desolate moors and rural communities, while much of it runs through a county where numerous existing preservation schemes will have mopped up most of the really committed enthusiast support. Add to this the lack of any practical operating base site on the S&C and the problems would daunt even the most optimistic suitor.

All such problems might yet be overcome, but one is left with the overwhelming impression that they had not really been thought through before floating the proposal. In his announcement, the Minister suggested that private enterprise would be far more able than BR to promote the line for tourist and recreational purposes. A survey has revealed that some 80% of its 300,000 passengers per year are travelling purely for the ride. This must be true of other lengthy sections of rural railway and the suggestion that BR is not in the business of carrying pleasure-riders casts doubt on their future. Asked if other lines such as the Central Wales and West Highland lines might be candidates for similar treatment, the Minister's reply was negative. One concludes that the S&C *is* therefore a special case. Lines with equal scenic and civil engineering attractions, but without the S&C's special character, would not receive the same consideration, one presumes. Perhaps the feeling is that it is railway enthusiasts who have made the fuss about the S&C and so it is up to them to do something about it. If so, the tables have effectively been turned on S&C supporters, for if 30 November arrives and there is no 'bridegroom' in the offing, the Minister and BR will be able to say that they offered a good deal and there were no takers.

After the May meeting, one could not help but feel that it had been something of a let-down. The much-vaunted announcement of a decision as to the line's future had been just another decision to delay a decision, but this time introducing a stronger hint that the outcome would be closure.

There can be little doubt that David Mitchell's own sympathies lay with keeping the S&C open, and that his announcement reflected departmental policy — some of it ill-considered or unconsidered. Came a summer Cabinet re-shuffle and Mitchell was gone. Perhaps his known sympathy for the S&C cause — and his rail interest in general — was a contributory factor.

His successor, Michael Portillo, then extended the deadline for objections to 30 November, in part to allow the TUCC more time to assemble its case from the large number of objections received. It was also announced that 'considerable numbers' of people had made purchase enquiries following the release by BR of a sale prospectus.

The sale prospectus was strongly criticised by the Friends of the Settle & Carlisle Line Association who found it 'Bristling with difficulty, hostility and restriction'. There were still many points left unclear. For instance, although there seems to be little difficulty expected over the negotiation of running rights into Carlisle, the prospectus appears to anticipate private operations terminating at Hellifield, although subsequently there has been some back-tracking over the possibility of through operation to Leeds. It is likely that any private operator would find through operation between Carlisle and Leeds essential.

After completion of experimental repairs to one arch of Ribblehead Viaduct, the estimate of likely cost was reduced from £4.3 million to £2.75 million, while traffic figures for the 1988 summer suggested that revenue figures were up to £1.7 million. Despite an increase in projected revenue and a reduction in projected repair costs, BR's updated financial case for closure still showed a loss of between £0.3 million and £1 million per year. The FoSCLA accused BR of 'adroit mathematical manipulation'.

Inevitably, even those who strongly support retention of the line by BR as the only practical option have had to concede that this is less and less likely, and to turn their attention to ways of making the best of the other options. On 26 October, the English Tourist Board lauched its Business Development Plan for the S&C, designed to guide interested parties, and eventual potential operators of the line, along the best commercial route.

To use a boxing metaphor, the fight for the S&C is now into the last round. The referee, in the shape of the Government, has tried to slow the fight down and to avoid making a decision on points. No one is throwing in the towel and there is everything to play for. If nothing else, the whole protracted S&C business will give future historians plenty to mull over, whatever the outcome when the final bell rings in 1989.

SMARDALE VIADUCT IN COURSE OF CONSTRUCTION.

More than five structures per mile –

looking at the engineering marvels of the Settle & Carlisle

P. M. Shaw

THE Settle & Carlisle line has become one of the most famous railway routes in the country in recent years. Such fame is attributed partly to the proposal to close a 72-mile stretch of main line, but mainly due to the outstanding scenery, and the engineering structures of the line itself.

When the Midland Railway was granted permission to build its own line north to Carlisle for Scottish traffic, it was intended to be every bit as good as the high-speed lines of the Midland's competitors to the east and west. This meant a line of shallow curves, gradients that were as moderate as possible, and as direct a route as could be made. The mountainous terrain of the Pennines meant building hundreds of structures to carry the track through hills,

and over streams, rivers and gulleys. On average, that meant over five structures a mile, and then only counting the ones that are given a bridge number. When culverts, signals, stations, and other buildings are added, the total becomes enormous.

The men responsible for the Settle & Carlisle were of that pioneering Victorian spirit that never doubted their ability to succeed. They were sorely tested from time to time, but were determined that their project would be a success on the grand scale.

The General Manager of the Midland was James Allport, and he was tired of the inferior treatment his passengers received from the London & North Western Railway, over whose metals they had to

travel on the line north of Ingleton over Shap to Carlisle. Negotiations about reasonable running powers met with failure, so the Midland decided to build its own line to Carlisle. An Act was passed in 1866 empowering the Midland to go ahead with the line from Settle to Carlisle. Realising it was about to lose trade, the London & North Western capitulated and sought an amicable arrangement with the Midland; and an arrangement was duly reached, but when the Midland applied for an Abandonment Bill, it was refused — the Settle & Carlisle had to be built!

Chief Engineer for the Midland was John Crossley, and he was assisted by John Sharland. These two men plotted the course of the line in detail. They could

make use of two principal valleys running south to north, those of the Ribble and the Eden, with links through Dentdale and Garsdale.

The first sod was cut near Anley House, to the south of Settle station. The line itself left the existing Skipton to Ingleton line at Settle Junction; two miles further north came Settle station.

Settle is a typical rural Midland station. There are two sizes of station on the line, known as 'small' and 'large'. As it serves a sizeable town, Settle is a 'large' station, meaning that it has a couple more rooms than the smaller variety.

The style is Gothic in appearance, solid and well-built. It is of stone construction throughout, with a cut and dressed finish. There was a large goods shed at Settle until very recently, now demolished to make room for an industrial estate, appropriately named The Sidings. To the rear of the main building is the old tank house, still with its tank on top; it is now used as a warehouse by a local firm. The station master's house, built to match the station, still stands by the up platform, although it is now privately owned. The down side

Below left:
Settle station: the 15.37 Carlisle-Leeds slows for the stop on 14 September 1982 behind Class 25/0 No 25042. *G. S. Cutts*

Below:
A northbound freight crosses Church Viaduct, Settle behind green painted Class 40 No 40106 on 8 September 1985. *W. A. Sharman*

waiting rooms were the same size at all stations, although some were wooden and others stone; the one at Settle is in stone.

Although Settle station is a listed building, British Rail has done little to look after it. The exterior is desperately in need of painting, and some of the inner rooms have extensive dry rot, with gaping holes in floors and ceilings.

Most people would probably not look for Mickey Mouse at Settle! For many years, a Mickey Mouse was attached to a lineside telegraph pole south of Dent (do not ask why!). He was so well-known to railway workers that when the telegraph poles were cut down and replaced by lineside telecommunications cabling, it was felt that Mickey could not be discarded, so

Above:
Sherrif Brow Viaduct, spanning the River Ribble. The 12.45 Carlisle-York DMU heads downgrade. *W. A. Sharman*

he found a new home at Settle. He can be seen looking down from one of the 'clover leaf' decorations above the ladies' room.

Settle station signalbox is still in situ, but only just. The signalling has been disconnected and the instruments removed. The signal arms have been taken down, and the bare poles look very odd. The final act of the sequence was lifting of the crossover in October 1986.

The first structure of any significance north of Settle station is Church Street Viaduct. This is to carry the line over the A65 Skipton to Kendal road, and forms an interruption in the mile-long, high embankment between Settle and Langcliffe. The viaduct takes its name from the parish church, in which there is a tablet of remembrance to the men who died building the line. There is an identical tablet in the tiny church of St Leonards, Chapel-le-Dale, near Ingleton, where over 100 men were buried.

The line runs through a deep rock cutting at Langcliffe. Trees overhang both sides of the cutting which can stay damp for months on end. In the autumn, this is the place to go if you want to see a train slip to a standstill! The falling leaves are squashed into a mushy pulp on the rails and it is not unusual to see even a Class 47 diesel locomotive come to a stand here. I recall the autumn of 1987 when a Class 31 locomotive on four coaches took 2hr to cover the section from Settle to Helwith Bridge. The driver and guard tried valiantly to make headway; the train setting back and taking a run, only to come to grief after 100yd. Both men got out to sand ½-mile of track by hand, but still the train could not get away, and the guard eventually hand-sanded right through to Stainforth school, nearly 1¼-mile in all!

Just after Langcliffe cutting is the site of the old lime works at Stainforth. Once boasting many sidings and a signalbox, all that remains is a huge quarry face and part of the old Hoffman kiln. The kiln is currently under investigation as part of the Ribblesdale trust project, which hopes to

renovate it as part of a plan to attract more visitors to the area. A small part of the kiln can be seen from the train, but it is enormous when explored on foot.

The first aqueduct we pass under is just after the kiln, and could easily escape the eye, being only a simple metal trough carrying a stream over the line.

Next comes Stainforth Tunnel, the first of many, but only a modest 120yd long. It passes under Taitlands, once home of local notaries but now a youth hostel.

The first sight of the River Ribble comes with the crossing of Sherrif Brow Viaduct, a graceful skew stone-built structure. It is quickly followed by the smaller Batty Wood Viaduct, again built of stone but with metal handrails instead of the more usual stone parapet.

Just around the corner we meet the River Ribble again, alongside another disused quarry. There are still the rails of a siding hidden in the undergrowth and, if you look in the river bed, you can see the concrete upright support that once carried a conveyor from quarry to siding.

We pass under the old bridge carrying the road to Austwick over both railway and river; this is Helwith Bridge, another listed building.

Immediately north of Helwith, the line crosses the Ribble for the last time, on 'Five Arches', a shallow stone bridge. This is a superb vantage point for photographers, combining many classical elements in one scene — a river, stone bridge, and Pen-y-ghent in the distance; it only needs the addition of a train to make it perfect!

Between Five Arches and Crag Hill farm is ½-mile of track that was like heaven to steam train crews in the past — for it was level ground. It is the only section on the flat between Settle Junction and Blea Moor, a distance of over 14 miles otherwise at a gradient of 1 in 100. To crews with a heavy train, it gave the chance to pick up a little speed — or simply to keep going! Foredale quarry sidings, with rope incline, used to be controlled by a signalbox at Helwith Bridge.

Horton in Ribblesdale is the next feature. It too once had an active quarry with exchange sidings. The last private locomotive was cut up on site in 1986. The small Midland signalbox remains, although with signalling disconnected. The station is one of the 'small' variety, and has seen a new lease of life since the Dalesman local passenger train service was reintroduced. Now served by 10 trains a day, it affords access to visitors, and provides a convenient means for local people to get into the towns. The Friends of the Settle-Carlisle Line Association adopted all eight reopened stations, and have painted them in red and cream livery. The gardens are slowly being restocked as well.

Continuing north, we pass two rows of obviously Midland railway cottages, but seemingly in the middle of nowhere! They are at Selside, where there used to be a signalbox. This one had a better fate than many, and is now at the Steamtown Railway Museum, Carnforth.

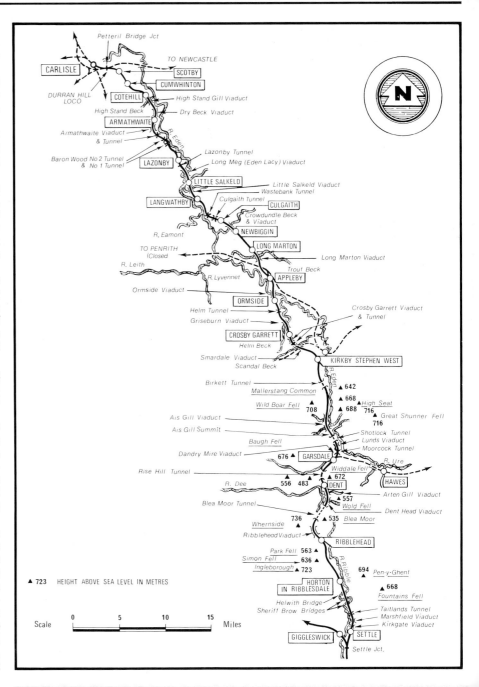

▲ 723   HEIGHT ABOVE SEA LEVEL IN METRES

Scale   0   5   10   15   Miles

Ribblehead station has only a southbound platform as the other was removed to provide easier access into the quarry sidings. Ballast stone from Ingleton was loaded into rail wagons here until January 1986. Engineers on the Eastern Region said this was the finest ballast available, but its use was sacrificed as part of the political strategy of running down the line for closure. The quarry was recently considered as a source of limestone for a flue gas de-sulphurisation plant at Drax power station, to curb acid emissions, but the National Parks lobby objected on environmental grounds.

The station master's house at Ribblehead is one of the most exposed homes in the area. It used to have a layer of slates on the side walls to keep out the horizontal rain; but the current school owners took the slates off and now have problems with damp walls! Those Midland builders knew the weather! Similarly, the Station Inn has a second, corrugated iron wall at the western end.

As we reach the head of Ribblesdale, the engineering features begin to take on a larger scale, as if to match the increasing size of the surrounding hills.

Ribblehead Viaduct is the most impressive structure on the whole line. It carries the nowadays singled track across a rather flat valley head, unlike most other viaducts, which span deep ravines. It took four years to build, reaching completion in 1874. It is a ¼-mile long, 105ft high, and has 24 arches. Every sixth pier is extra large, and called a king pier.

The proposal to close the line seems to have revolved around the cost of repairs to this one viaduct. As it is in such an exposed position, the winter weather creates special maintenance problems. The asphalt layer that forms the waterproof membrane perished long ago, and the water percolating through into the piers causes the damage. It freezes and thaws in cycles, and the formation of ice causes the stone to crack. Other cracks now run round the join between arches and spandrels. Some repairs have been carried out to keep it safe for passage of trains, and the track was singled in 1985, but little has really been done to eradicate the heart of the problem; new waterproofing would be a big help.

Estimates for repairs have varied wildly over the years, from BR's original claim of

£6 million, to an independent estimate of only £1 million. Most groups accept another independent estimate of £2.1-£2.7 million. The English Heritage Trust has pledged £1 million towards repairs, and other funding is being sought. The viaduct is a scheduled Ancient Monument, and fully deserves to be properly repaired. It looks impressive as you see it from the train, but the sheer scale of the civil engineering only becomes fully apparent as you stand underneath it. Viewed from the valley floor, it is an awesome feeling to think that it was built by men with virtually no mechanical equipment. It brings to mind the phrase of the late Rt Rev Eric Treacy, Bishop of Wakefield, who said that the Settle-Carlisle was one of the wonders of Northern England, on a par with York Minster and Hadrians Wall.

Just beyond the viaduct is the isolated signalbox at Blea Moor. It once had a pair of cottages, a detached house and a water tank for company but now only the dilapidated house remains. The signalbox is over a mile from the nearest road, but it

must seem like 10 miles to a signalman going on duty at 06.00 on a cold, wet winter's day.

Although isolated, Blea Moor does see its fair share of interesting traffic. The early morning commuter train from Ribblehead to Leeds comes out from Skipton empty, and crosses over here. It also brings the signalman mail and two jerry cans of drinking water! Electricity finally reached the box a couple of years ago; before then, lighting was by Calor gas. With the arrival of mains power also came electric radiators, although the coal stove is still pressed into use when the weather is really cold.

The frequent use of the Settle & Carlisle line by trains diverted from the West Coast main line by engineering work means that a standby locomotive is often parked in the loop at Blea Moor, ready to rescue trains whose locomotives have failed.

Signals controlled by this signalbox are fairly typical of others on the line, a mixture of colour-light and semaphore. The down distant is a colour-light, as is the

Top left:
Bridge 71 — an aqueduct — south of Blea Moor Tunnel. Passing underneath is an up freight behind Class 40 No 40040, on 11 June 1975. *J. H. Cooper-Smith*

Above left:
Kell Beck Culvert — the largest on the line — south of Dent station. *P. M. Shaw*

Above:
It took five years to build Dent Head Viaduct from blue limestone. An up freight crosses on 14 May 1973. *J. H. Cooper-Smith*

down home, and the down starter is a tall metal-post semaphore. The route indicator at the north end of the single line is a ground level panel showing 'DM' for down main, or 'UL' for up loop. On the up line is a unique banner repeating distant at the north end of the tunnel — some 2¼ miles before its home signal. At the south entrance to the tunnel is a beautiful old semaphore distant with a wooden post; it is one of only two left on the line — the other

is at Garsdale. The up home is a semaphore, with a bracket semaphore for the loop. There is not a starter on the up line; one would be useful though, to increase line capacity on diversion days, as the long section between Blea Moor and Settle Junction can cause delays. Other signals are an up loop semaphore starter; a ground-sited electric light shunt for moving out of the loop northwards on to the up main, and a Limit of Shunt on the up main. What were the down loop and engineers' sidings are now clipped out of use. The quarry siding at Ribblehead is controlled by a ground frame at Ribblehead, with an interlock to Blea Moor.

Just before plunging into Blea Moor Tunnel, the line is crossed by another aqueduct. This is a substantial stone structure, with a stepped bed to allow the stream to run downhill. It also carries a bridle-path to one side and a footpath at the other.

Blea Moor Tunnel is another of the engineering marvels. It is 2,629yd long (1½ miles). It was originally intended to be

absolutely straight, but this would have left a sheer cutting at the south end, so the first ¼-mile is curved. There are now three air shafts, the deepest being almost 400ft. The tunnel was cut from 12 faces; two ends, and five shafts, each with two faces. Two shafts were blocked up on completion. Part of the tunnel is brick-lined and part is bare rock. The remains of the trolley track over the moor can be clearly seen, as can the anchor stones of an old winding house. Various pieces of ironwork also sit on the moor, including vent covers that have been recently replaced.

The line emerges from the north portal of Blea Moor Tunnel into the county of Cumbria, and rapidly crosses two more large viaducts, Dent Head and Arten Gill, both scheduled Ancient Monuments. Dent Head has 10 spans, and Arten Gill, 11, the latter being a tall, graceful structure with tapering piers built of a bluish limestone known as Dent marble.

The track level is about 500ft above the valley floor. The journey along Dentdale is perhaps the most breathtaking section of

all, giving views of both railway and scenery that are strikingly beautiful.

Kell Beck waterfall is just by the line and, as this beck tumbles down from Great Knoutberry hill, it is carried under the line in what can only be described as a most astonishing culvert. It has an elaborate, ornamental entrance and exit, and is stepped inside. To put such a stunning dressed finish to a culvert shows how the Midland viewed its new route. Even though few people would ever see it, workmanship and design had to be of the best. This culvert is the most decorative, but all those on the route are attractively finished.

Dent station claims two records; it is the highest main line station in England, at 1,150ft above sea level; and the station master's house was reputedly the first in the country to have double glazing.

The cutting just past the station used to be a hazard in winter, as it trapped snow blowing from the fells. Nowadays, the afforestation seems to trap the snow. Along Dentdale there is a double row of

upright sleepers above the line to act as snow fences.

Rise Hill is the second longest tunnel on the route, at 1,213yd. It has two air shafts. The northern portal is an oddity in that it is very plain, without any embellishments.

Between Rise Hill and Garsdale are a series of small overbridges that represent those all along the line; some of brick, others of stone. While they may only give access from a field on one side of the track to the moor on the other side, they too are well-built.

The highest water troughs in the world used to be on this length, but now only the splashers and marker posts remain. The markers are concrete posts about 8ft tall, with a ladder up one side for the lampman to climb and hang a lamp on the bracket, indicating to train crews the location of the troughs after dark. There was a large tank house by the line, and it was fed by a stream running down the fellside. If you follow the stream uphill, the remains of an old dam can clearly be seen. There is a little hut with a stove in, to keep a man warm as he stopped the dam freezing over. The area was surrounded by heavy iron railings which have all fallen down now, except one length next to the gate — still securely padlocked to this day!

Garsdale station is different to all the others as it had an island platform at one side, as this was the junction for the branch line to Hawes. The signalbox on the down platform is operational, but now only used when trains are diverted over the line. The waiting room on the down platform used to contain a harmonium, and the vicar from Garsdale village held services there. The old tankhouse also had its social uses, as the local dance hall!

The trackbed of the Hawes branch can be seen diverging east by the sidings. To the west of the line, opposite the sidings, are the remains of the old turntable; famed for the time when an engine was caught broadside by the wind in 1900, and spun like a top for 2hr. Recently the traverser was sold to the Keighley and Worth Valley railway who wanted to put its own turntable back into use. On hearing of the proposed move, the National Parks Committee applied for a Building Preservation

Notice; this was granted, so the KWVR is unable to move the traverser. The Preservation Notice is an interim, holding process, until the Secretary of State for the Environment decides whether to 'list' the turntable.

Moorcock or Dandry Mire Viaduct was intended to be an embankment, but the mire absorbed so much earth that a viaduct had to be built instead. Just alongside is the Mount Zion Primitive Methodist Chapel of 1876, with its regular congregation of six souls.

Moorcock Tunnel, 98yd in length, is quickly followed by Lunds Viaduct, and the quarry from which the stone was obtained is directly underneath.

Next comes one of the inexplicable features of the line; the metal footbridge at Grisedale crossing. This is a small, unmanned drovers' crossing, but it also has a fine, angled footbridge. The number of people in the area can be counted on the fingers of one hand, and certainly never

Above left:
Remains of a snow fence on the fell-side above Dent station. *P. M. Shaw*

Above:
Dent station is 1,150ft above sea level. *P. M. Shaw*

needed this bridge, but it stands proud for all to see.

Through Shotlock Hill Tunnel, 106yd, and we reach the summit of the line at Ais Gill, 1,169ft above sea level. There were refuge sidings and a signalbox here in steam days. Both have now gone; the sidings for scrap, but the signalbox to the Midland Railway Trust at Butterley.

Below:
Moorcock Viaduct, across Dandry Mire. Originally this was to be an embankment, but the failure to find sound footings resulted in the construction of the viaduct. The 10.27 Skipton-Carlisle DMU crosses on 23 August 1986. *W. A. Sharman*

Once 'over the top', the line rapidly descends into the Eden valley; and the story of bridges, tunnels, viaducts and culverts is repeated all the way to Carlisle.

There is Hangman's Bridge, where legend says a platelayer committed suicide. Then there is the still thriving railway community at Appleby, with goods shed, station, signalbox, engineer's yard — and the only branch line, to the army base at Warcop.

There are level crossings at Culgaith and Low House; and there is the electronic train describer in Howe & Co's signalbox. This links the Settle & Carlisle to the 'high-tech' world of Carlisle power signalbox.

A ride over the line by train, or a journey of exploration by car and foot, reveals a never ending selection of engineering achievements of the highest order. Some are on the grand scale, such as Ribblehead Viaduct or Blea Moor Tunnel; some are smaller, such as the intricacies of

a culvert; others are merely reminders of a bygone age, like the semaphore signalling. Whatever your particular interest, it will be represented somewhere between Settle and Carlisle.

One of the more esoteric items is the stone on Smardale Viaduct. It is inscribed 'This last stone was laid by Agness Crossley, 8th June 1875'. If Agness Crossley came back to see the line today, she could still be proud of the skill her husband displayed in building it.

Above left:
The 110yd Crosby Garrett Viaduct. The 11.50 Glasgow-Nottingham crosses on 12 August 1981. *W. A. Sharman*

Above:
Smardale Viaduct on 1 July 1982. The 16.05 Leeds-Carlisle heads north behind Class 47/4 No 47538. *John Checkley*

Below:
The south end of the 106yd Shotlock Hill Tunnel, between Garsdale and Ais Gill. Note the drains for water coming off the fells. *P. M. Shaw*

BIRKETT CUTTING.

Look back at the last decade

Left:
Effectively, BR's rationale for maintaining the S&C, once the West Coast main line was electrified in 1974, was the need to route partially fitted/unfitted through freight trains over the line for operational reasons. These scheduled workings ceased or were diverted by May 1983. Class 40 No 40033 toils upgrade towards Ais Gill summit with a southbound freight on 29 August 1978. *John E. Oxley*

Above:
BR's InterCity 125 units have made appearances over the S&C on charter or special workings only. The first examples were diverted East Coast services in 1980. This shows a special run for BR's publicity purposes on 16 May 1981, the IC125 unit running from Leeds-Howe & Co's Sidings and back, with stops *en route* for official photographs. On the return trip, the unit passes Culgaith, with the unique, untypical (for the S&C) station building showing behind the front power car. *S. McGahon*

Right:
The 06.30 Carlisle-Leeds crosses Arten Gill Viaduct on 4 July 1987, and illustrates the length of train required to accommodate the many passengers attracted to the beauties of the Settle & Carlisle in the last few years. Motive power is Class 47/4 No 47424. *Peter J. Robinson*

Above left:
From May 1976, the remaining Anglo-Scottish express trains were withdrawn from the route, to be replaced by daytime Nottingham-Glasgow services. These ceased in May 1982; one such is powered by a Class 45, northbound near Kirkby Stephen. *M. Dunnett*

Inset:
From May 1982, there were two Leeds-Carlisle trains each way only. This shows Kirkby Stephen station on 25 May 1983 with Class 31/4 No 31406 on the 15.37 Carlisle-Leeds. *Kevin Hughes*

Left:
Disruptions to West Coast main line working have seen frequent diversions of the route's trains over the S&C. On 4 March 1983, a derailment at Warrington resulted in air braked freight trains running via Ais Gill, such as this Mossend-Severn Tunnel Junction service, with Class 47/3 No 47317 leading a variety of modern wagons near Birkett Common. *C. Addis*

Above:
In 1975, the Yorkshire Dales National Park sponsored the 'Dales Rail' excursions for walkers and local passengers and these trains reintroduced a service to intermediate stations. Here is one such train returning on 3 August 1985, made up of portions for Preston and Leeds and seen crossing Arten Gill Viaduct. *Keith Smith*

Right:
From July 1986, timetabled local trains reappeared on the Settle & Carlisle. A Leeds-Carlisle stopping train has just passed Culgaith on 13 July 1988. *Brian Dobbs*

BARON WOOD CUTTING.

The resurgence of steam on the S&C

Joan Jackson

THE TRAIL of white steam and black smoke spreads out against the moors, as distant trains struggle up the 1 in 100 gradient of this craggy terrain; whistles faintly echoing in the desolation. The landscape dwarfs the railway with its majestic viaducts, high embankments, long tunnels and graceful bridges marching along the Pennines from Settle to Carlisle. Hordes of photographers file across the fields, two or more cameras apiece, with much camaraderie and rivalry, to record the passing of steam. Twenty years ago, as today, the steam fever gripped with a desperation born of despair. On Saturday, 11 August 1968, all my train-spotting friends went into mourning for the end of steam on BR. No more Long Meg-Widnes anhydrite trains, not even a humble 'Black 5' left; nothing for the future but faceless diesels and electrics.

Unfortunately, the 15 guinea fare to travel on the last steam train over the S&C was way beyond our pockets — even if we could have got tickets for such a sought-after event. So we persuaded an indulgent parent that there would be no traffic out in the wilds at Ais Gill. He was not amused to find himself driving at a snail's pace on a rare, hot English summer day; desperately trying to find a parking space at Ais Gill summit.

It was unthinkable then that, 10 years later, on 25 March 1978, *Green Arrow* would be hauling the 'Norfolkman' charter train northbound over the same line. This time, the weather was more typical as the Gresley 2-6-2 struggled up to Ribblehead through the snow, dropping to 22mph; much to the delight of the photographers chasing her by road. Named in honour of Bill Harvey, ex-LNER man, one-time shedmaster at Norwich, who had overseen the locomotive's restoration to working order, *Green Arrow* spearheaded a revival of steam on this most challenging of lines. Before this, *Flying Scotsman* had been

over the line. She was the only locomotive permitted to run on BR after the end of steam and, on 26 October 1968, this famous engine pulled the 'Moorlands' over the S&C. Then, in 1976, the centenary of the line had been celebrated by *Flying Scotsman* and *Hardwicke* running into Settle station from Hellifield, to much acclaim.

During 1978, excitement mounted as other locomotive owners applied to BR for permission to run their engines over the S&C. Sadly, that renowned railway photographer, Eric Treacy, the Bishop of Wakefield, died at Appleby station while waiting for *Evening Star* hauling the 'Border Venturer' on 13 May that year.

A memorial service at Appleby station was held for Eric Treacy on 30 September 1978, involving two trains: the 'Lord Bishop' with *Flying Scotsman* and the 'Bishop Treacy' with *Evening Star*, reputedly a favourite of his, attending the ceremony. *Clan Line* was also involved. Considerable planning went into the movement of the locomotives to avoid

Below left:
'A4' Pacific No 4498 *Sir Nigel Gresley* **on Ribblehead Viaduct with the 'Cumbrian Mountain Pullman'. The semaphore signals stand out against Whernside and rows of photographers brave the biting wind. The signals have gone but the scaffolding is a familiar sight as repairs are carried out to the viaduct. 28 November 1981.** *K. J. C. Jackson*

Below:
LMS '5' No 5407 shows her paces for the train passengers during a photograhic run-past over the Moorcock Viaduct at Garsdale. Their safety is protected by the signal and train stewards. This was an early appearance of the Pullman set of coaches which introduced a touch of luxury to the service. The '5' handled the heavy train single-handed. 2 May 1981. *David E. Jackson*

Bottom:
'West Country' Pacific No 34092 *City of Wells* **hurries across the 'sylvan dell' of Crowdundle. One Skipton driver thought her good for branch line DMU diagrams while another got some very creditable performances out of her! 10 December 1983.** *K. J. C. Jackson*

preparation for the stiff climb of almost 15 miles from Settle Junction to Blea Moor summit. Stringent safety checks were enforced and each locomotive had to have a cold examination and a steam test before every run. There were to be three BR representatives on the footplate at all times, driver, fireman and traction inspector. All this costs money and, for long journeys, two or more crews are needed.

Yet steam working gathered momentum. The A4 Locomotive Society ran the 'Aire-Eden' charter train from Leeds to Carlisle on 21 October 1978 with 'A4' Pacific *Sir Nigel Gresley* and the 'Moorlander' back over the line the next day. The crews soon adapted to the 'A4' which is very free-steaming. Then the planned trains for 1979 were shelved because the Penmanshiel Tunnel disaster on the East Coast route between Newcastle and Edinburgh meant that there were diversions of East Coast Anglo-Scottish trains over the S&C and it was not possible to schedule steam workings with their necessary water-stops. In the old days, there were water troughs at Garsdale

Top:
Flashback to BR's Last Steam Train: LMS Class 5s Nos 44871 and 44781 south of Ribblehead on the southbound run of 11 August 1968. What a pity a commemorative special was not operated in 1988! *Gerald T. Robinson*

Above:
Steamtown Railway Museum at Carnforth re-living its days as an LMS running shed in providing stabling for the visiting *Duchess of Hamilton*, which had hauled the 'Red Rose' special train from York. 21 August 1982. *K. J. C. Jackson*

costly light engine workings. John Bellamy, Chairman of the Merchant Navy Locomotive Preservation Society, recalls *Clan Line* working the 'Citadel' from York to Carlisle on 23 September, in order to be in position to haul the returning 'Lord Bishop' special from Armathwaite to Hellifield.

John Bellamy was impressed with the way that the enginemen handled an unfamiliar locomotive. He was advised not

to use water treatment because the Carlisle water was good. However, on the way up the bank, she was priming badly. The late Fred Prickett, the MNLPS owner's representative, with more than 40 years' experience of the footplate at Nine Elms, was very pleased with the way Driver Jimmy Mclellan and Inspector George 'Geordie' Gordon handled the situation. One of the potential problems in opening up the line to preserved locomotives was that Carlisle, Skipton and Leeds men would all be expected to handle 'foreign' engines on this most testing of routes. In steam days, engines were road tested on the 'Long Drag'. However, in steam days the regular train service tended to be lightly loaded in comparison to the 12, 13 or even 14-coach trains used in preservation.

Another factor was that most preserved locomotives saw only irregular working, were ageing and either languished in museums or ran up and down short lengths of track. This was hardly adequate

and water columns at most stations, as well as at Blea Moor. Now special arrangements have to be made for water. At Appleby, Eden Vale supplies water from its dairy, which adjoins the line; while, at Garsdale, there is a settling tank fed by two streams; this was the former supply to the two water columns and cottages.

In the early days, volunteers from Steamtown Railway Centre manned the hoses at Garsdale. Then Bill Allan, a regular traveller, took on the job and he tried to improve the flow of water and is

Right:
Bulleid 'West Country' No 34092 *City Of Wells* **passes the wooden posted Midland distant signal for Blea Moor outer home, on the up road. 7 April 1984.** *K. J. C. Jackson*

Below:
Duchess of Hamilton **crossing Dent Head Viaduct with a Carlisle train,** *en route* **to Ayr Open Day. Her path had been smoothed by the passage of a Sandite train the previous day, to help prevent the annual autumn problem of slipping on wet, leaf-strewn rails. 29 October 1983.**
Joan Jackson

constantly on the look-out for new improvements. He is a familiar figure today, with his young son, servicing almost every steam train that stops at Garsdale.

1980 saw the start of the 'Cumbrian Mountain Expresses'. Dreamed up by David Ward of BR's InterCity and Bernard Staite, Chairman of the Steam Locomotive Operators' Association, and no doubt inspired by the success of BR's 'Cumbrian Coast Express', it soon gripped the imagination of the steam enthusiast. The first train advertised 120 miles of steam haulage from Carnforth to Skipton and thence to Carlisle over the full length of the S&C. There was a buffet service and

Above left:
LMS '5' No 5407 and 'Jubilee' No 5690 *Leander* below the slopes of Pen-y-ghent as they approach Horton-in-Ribblesdale. 29 May 1982.

Left:
Ex-Southern No 850 *Lord Nelson* at Smardale, far from its onetime haunts. Not designed for this sort of terrain, No 850 performed well with careful handling. *Both: K. J. C. Jackson*

full dining facilities. In those days the set of coaches came from Blackpool.

It was first thought unlikely that steam would run under the overhead electric wires at Carlisle and first thoughts were that the engine would come off at Durran Hill, just outside the city, and a pilot locomotive used to haul the train in and out of the station. However, it was decided to proceed with caution and with strict attention to avoid the engines blowing off steam and so causing flash-overs which can damage the catenary and insulators.

On 19 January 1980, 'Black 5' No 5305 worked the 'Cumbrian Mountain Express' to Skipton where *Sir Nigel Gresley* was waiting to haul the first 'CME' over the 'Long Drag', returning with the south-bound train the following week. SLOA Marketing organised the trains which were provided with stewards to attend to the comfort of passengers and take care of their safety at water-stops, where they could photograph the train.

It soon became evident that there was enormous sustained interest in steam

Above left:
Seeming to be on top of the world *Flying Scotsman* drifts across the stark, stone-turned viaduct with the southbound 'Cumbrian Mountain Express'. Only the ferns reveal that it is not winter in this bleak terrain. 22 July 1981. *Joan Jackson*

Above:
Duchess of Hamilton takes water at Garsdale the 'modern' way — through a gravity-fed hosepipe. The volunteer support crew check round while their mentor takes a break in the rare sunshine with train manager and architect of many successful steam enterprises, Bernard Staite (in dark glasses). 9 June 1984. *K. J. C. Jackson*

excursions over the S&C. They were clearly a success and more trains were added. There were many regular travellers who never missed a train and took an interest in locomotive performance. They recorded both the sound and the output and liked to compare the different locomotives. 1980 was the year of the Rainhill 150 celebrations and there was enormous excitement when the veteran North British 0-6-0 locomotive *Maude* en route from Scotland to Rainhill travelled over the line on a lovely day in May. Unheard of crowds of photographers charted her progress.

As more locomotives were added to the list of runners, interest grew and a fine day would see some intensive car rallying along the narrow, twisting roads between the drystone walls. Every field and vantage-point seemed to be full of earnest photographers from all over the country. Tired of having his lineside field taken over, one farmer took the ultimate revenge. With perfect timing, he got out his muck-spreader and the field emptied like lightning. It is a brave person who ventures near that farm. The farmer also has an impressive bull!

Left:
Flying Scotsman racing towards Shotlock Hill Tunnel through the deceptively gentle-looking summit countryside in haytime with the 'Cumbrian Mountain Pullman'. For much of the year, mist hangs low over the hills and rain and gales lash the line. 27 July 1983. *K. J. C. Jackson*

A friendly rivalry sprang up between the support teams for the preserved locomotives working over the S&C, with unofficial races to Blea Moor in the down direction and Ais Gill in the up direction. 'A4' *Sir Nigel Gresley* and the 'Duchess' alternated in doing the honours, with the 'Duchess' wearing the Blue Riband with great pride in May 1983, for the southbound run from Appleby to Ais Gill summit. Another favourite, the green 'A4' *Union of South Africa,* excited even more interest and holds the now unbeatable record from Settle Junction to the summit. 'Unbeatable 'because as the track deteriorated, permanent way slacks were introduced which severely hampered the 'races'.

One eagerly awaited event was the appearance of the Midland Compound No 1000 in February 1983, double-headed with *Leander.* It was bitterly cold and the weather did its worst. A howling gale whipped up a blizzard. I froze in horizontally blowing snow at Dent Head to catch a glimpse of No 1000. The train was very late

because of diversions of West Coast Main Line trains over the S&C and this delayed watering of the special at Hellifield. There was no Garsdale stop that day.

The enginemen working over the S&C became accustomed to a wide variety of motive power. Representatives of Southern 'West Country', 'Lord Nelson' and 'King Arthur' classes travelled over the line. Once the sophistication of Bulleid Light Pacific *City of Wells* had been mastered, she performed excellently as did *Lord Nelson,* providing the latter was supplied with good coal and received an

appropriate firing technique suited to its long firebox. 'King Arthur' *Sir Lamiel* presented more problems as her injectors work the opposite way to more modern ones. Her first trip over the line was as pilot to 'Black Five' No 5407 because of fears about *Sir Lamiel's* performance which happily proved to be groundless. The 'King Arthur went on to give several sparkling solo performances. Of course, chances cannot be taken with these steam runs as a breakdown is costly in terms of lost time, missed connections and consequent delay to following trains.

Above right:
Evening Star, on a rare visit to the S&C, runs through the former Long Marton station, typical of many of the small Midland stations on the line, in the gentler scenery north of Appleby. 23 April 1984. *Joan Jackson*

Right:
Very appropriate motive power as Midland Compound No 1000 pilots 'Jubilee' No 5690 Leander with the 'Cumbrian Mountain Pullman' through Lazonby station, with its old goods shed and water column; the latter has since gone. 12 February 1983. *Joan Jackson*

Below:
Flying Scotsman and support coach pass Dent signalbox *en route* for Scotland. From Carlisle, the Pacific worked a train the following day to Ayr in readiness for the Open Day a week later. Unfortunately, Dent signalbox is no longer there. 21 October 1983. *Joan Jackson*

It is sad that no Great Western engines have been able to join the privileged fleet of steam locomotives working over the S&C. *Clun Castle* travelled the line in 1967 but, today, there are problems of satisfactory clearances under the overhead electric wires for the 'King' and of adequate cylinder clearances en route to the line for 'Halls' and 'Manors'.

Gradually, the character of the steam workings has changed from the early enthusiast specials, to the introduction of the 'Cumbrian Mountain Expresses', to today's luxury 'Pennine Pullman' with its silver service, for a memorably different day out. All sorts of travellers patronise these trains from the tired executive, looking for a new experience, to the local signalman who has saved up to celebrate a birthday or anniversary. They all have one thing in common: their interest in riding over the S&C behind a well-turned out steam locomotive, be it *Flying Scotsman* or a 'Black 5'. Whoever travels, they will have a day to remember with a very friendly atmosphere.

Steam working has become more efficient over the years. Watering at Skipton from *Flying Scotsman's* spare tender was rather frustrating with a platform end water column on full view, yet this was out of order! So the 'CME' ceased to run to/from Skipton and the engines were swapped at Hellifield instead to save time in case of delay or failure, and so ensure that passengers caught their connections further south. William Baines of Ingleton provided a water tanker, in order to supply water to the engine at the

Above:
LMS '8F' No 48151 runs briskly downhill past the site of Crosby Garrett station with a Leeds-Carlisle special. 25 June 1988.
K. J. C. Jackson

Below:
Carlisle Citadel station plays host to 'Black 5' No 44767 with its Stephenson link valve gear, as she waits with support vehicles for the train to arrive from Edinburgh, which she took to Keighley over the S&C. Running under the wires is carefully monitored and kept to an absolute minimum to avoid flash-overs. 6 September 1986. *K. J. C. Jackson*

Hellifield stop. Next followed the use of a road tanker with water pumped into the locomotive tender from the tanker standing on the over bridge at Long Preston.

1988 has seen the twentieth anniversary of the end of steam on BR and the tenth anniversary of its return to the line. The 'Cumbrian Mountain Express' returned and *Mallard* celebrated the golden jubilee of its world speed record by taking a train over the S&C. Many things have changed. Early problems have been resolved, and some locomotives have undergone major overhaul to receive the coveted seven-year certificate for main line running on BR. Today's footplatemen step aboard a fully prepared locomotive, enjoy their turn and step off again, leaving the volunteer workforce to dispose of the engine and correct any faults before the next run. For the BR enginemen, steam is a much sought-after turn.

In fact, the involvement of volunteer labour is essential for the continuation of steam workings on BR. Even so, the use of steam on the main line is costly. For many of the jobs involved in maintaining a steam locomotive, you would be unable to find willing paid labourers. Scraping grease and carbon from engine frames is dirty, tedious and time-consuming work, but it is necessary during preparation for a major overhaul in order to examine components thoroughly and to make things easier for fitting parts. The overhaul itself is a lengthy task but once the locomotive is restored to sound running order, the joy is inestimable, too, as the first match is lit and the needle on the boiler pressure gauge comes round to the red mark and the engine blows off safely. For the volunteers it is a pleasure to present a well-prepared engine for the BR crews to operate.

Help in all this from the steam museums and from BR depots is vital. Steamtown Railway Centre at Carnforth, the National Railway Museum, York and the Keighley and Worth Valley Railway all provide locomotives that pull the steam excursions over the S&C. Their pits, workshops, preparation and disposal facilities are all essential for continued steam operation. BR depot at Upperby, Carlisle, on the site of the old steam shed, provides a second home for lay-over periods and the men there take a great interest in the 'steamers'.

The return of steam has brought great publicity during the period the line has been faced with closure while local hostelries and bed and breakfast establishments have benefited financially from the influx of visitors. The S&C is a tourist attraction in itself, but with steam trains, it is a winner. It must be hoped that the line can be saved. The goodwill between BR and the locomotive operators has resulted in a successful joint marketing operation to fill trains. Obviously, there must be doubt as to the future running of steam without this close co-operation. If politicians and accountants allow a private bid to be successful, a new working relationship must be achieved for the safe and profitable operation of steam on the S&C.

DENT HEAD VIADUCT.

The Settle & Carlisle
its mystery and majesty

*As a cameo of the Settle & Carlisle, we have chosen a very special piece of writing, from the late **Derek Cross,** a renowned railway photographer and commentator, who died in May 1984. It was submitted as an article for publication in April 1976 at the time of the S&C's centenary and presents a portrait of the line from a distinctive writer with a particular affection for this remarkable stretch of railway.*

WOOMPH! The 'Jubilee' class 4-6-0 hauling the 'Thames-Forth' express blasted into Baron Wood No 1 Tunnel. A few moments of darkness and then it was out again into the spring sunlight, with tantalising glimpses of the River Eden below, filled with fat salmon and cloaked with spring green trees, then another patch of darkness through Baron Wood No 2 Tunnel and the fish course was served. A friend and I were travelling south from Edinburgh on what was then the 'Thames-Forth' express and having lunch in the newly restored restaurant car sharing our table with two stately looking clerics, one of whom sampled his fish and turned to the other with the immortal remark, 'This is the piece of cod which passeth all understanding'. It was unfair, as in those far-off days you got a four-course lunch for under 50p and there was a through train from Edinburgh to St Pancras, while there was also a Waverley Route for it to travel on. There are so many memories of that beautiful, but at the same time frightening line, quite simply man's greatest challenge to nature in the raw that this country has seen. Every railway has its mystique but the S&C had an aura all its own. If my irreverent memory from student days has

lasted in my mind it is only one of many. Others include the mind-bending beat of a '9F' 2-10-0 being thrashed out on the 'Long Meg' anhydrite train through Birkett Tunnel, the cold, sepulchral gloom of Blea Moor Tunnel, summer breezes dancing pavannes among the moorland grass surrounding Dent and, always, the sight of great hills on either side of this remarkable line; for it *is* a remarkable line.

It is a line seen best from the train, the superb crossing and re-crossing of the Ribble in the Stainforth Gorge, the vast upland vistas on the climb past Selside and the views down Dentdale on an autumn morning, not to mention what to me is the loveliest section of all, the drop down the Eden Valley south of Armathwaite. Such

was its majesty . . . what of its mystery? The Helm wind, that strange turbulent screaming monster that tears down Edendale from Cross Fell; the eerie echoes of Blea Moor Tunnel, the two terrible accidents on either side of Ais Gill summit, made all the worse by the elements and the high isolated country. For all its triumphs and its tragedies, why was this line across the spine of England ever built? The answer is short and rude . . . to put the lordly London & North Western Railway in its place at Carlisle. For a short while this the Midland Railway achieved.

It was a line born in turmoil, built with a terrible toll of human tragedy through accidents in the workings and a smallpox outbreak at Ribblehead. The line was no status symbol, no deliberate gesture of defiance against the elements or geology: it was brought about by the sheer bloody-mindedness of the 'Euston Confederacy'. In the 1850s, traffic from the Leeds area to Scotland was carried by way of the Little North Western line which the Midland had acquired, by way of the improbably named Clapham Junction to Ingleton. Now here was the snag, for beyond Ingleton that lovely line up the Lune Valley (now closed) was owned by the LNWR and for a while, what was known in these days as a 'working agreement' was in force . . . but to the great benefit of the LNWR! Then things went wrong, very wrong, culminating in a separation at Ingleton whereby the Midland had one station and the LNWR another . . . at opposite ends of a

superb stone viaduct. Passengers from Yorkshire to the north had to detrain at one station and walk across the viaduct. Considering the vast amount of luggage conveyed by travellers in the last century, and all the pomp and rectitude of their clothing, it must have been a somewhat nerve wracking experience in the teeth of the usual Pennine gale. This state of affairs lasted far longer than it should have done, but a century and a decade ago the Midland and the LNWR were like two fighting dogs that, if separated at one point, promptly joined battle at another. Things came to a head when a high Midland official — rumour has it that it was James Allport himself — having detrained at sis-alpine Ingleton, negotiated the walk across the viaduct, re-trained at trans-alpine Ingleton, only to be turfed out into the cold yet again at Tebay to wait for an LNWR local train to get to Carlisle. This was too much and so the germ of an independent line from Leeds to Carlisle was born.

It was a thought but, like the chorus of witches in *Dido and Aeneas* . . . 'tell us, tell us how shall this be done'? Between Settle and Carlisle there were two valleys running roughly north/south, the Ribble from the Settle end and the Eden from Carlisle. So far, so good, but between these two valleys the line had to cross the watershed of Northern England with Wensleydale draining to the east and Dentdale draining to the west. This, coupled with some very complex geology ranging from hard granites to shattered shales and a goodly helping of limestone thrown in, comprised the problem. Right from the word go, something of the mystery of the S&C crops up in one Sharland, reputedly a Tasmanian engineer. Various learned people have attempted to debunk Sharland's part in the construction of the line but I feel that this is based on a misconception. Sharland was not an engineer, he was a surveyor. Just as the modern engineers tend to debunk geologists so their Victorian ancestors tended to ignore surveyors. I worked in the Antipodes for a number of years and am convinced that the Settle & Carlisle line could never have been conceived by anyone who had not known the wide open spaces and great ranges of Tasmania. The whole breadth of vision was something alien to the native surveyors/engineers of a century ago, sound as they were. Only one other line in the country tackled similar country in the same bold way. This was the Highland Railway, significantly surveyed and built by Joseph Mitchell, a native of Inverness to whom hills were home and towns hell. The more I know of the S&C and the land forms it passes through, the more sure I am that the survey was the work of Sharland. He may have driven in his last peg and been politely asked by the engineers to take himself elsewhere, and he certainly died before the line was completed, worn out, so it is said, by the Pennine winds, the snows and frosts of winter and the bottomless bogs after a thaw.

The route of the Settle and Carlisle has an anomaly that has puzzled me for as long as I have known it. The route up Ribblesdale was logical and, compared with the line via Shap, reasonably graded, though there was a lot of 1 in 100. Having got to Ribblehead, why not follow the route of what is now the Hawes/Ingleton road to the east of Widdale Fell and then bend to the west some mile or so short of Hawes and follow what became the Hawes branch to Garsdale? The summit here would have been 1,120ft and, though wet in places, there was nothing to stop building a railway on a reasonably stable foundation. It would have avoided such horrors as Blea Moor Tunnel, Ribblehead and Arten Gill Viaducts and Rise Hill Tunnel. Such a route might have been slightly longer, but it would have been infinitely easier and cheaper to build. It would also have removed the most spectacular scenic length of the whole line. Not that the Midland Railway would have minded that as its purpose was to get to Carlisle as cheaply as possible. . . . Did I say *cheaply?* It was the most expensive line ever built in England, costing well over £6 million, much to the directors' chagrin.

For some reason, the line from Ribble-head to Garsdale (originally Hawes Junction) was built *over* Ribblehead, *under* Blea Moor, and *over* Denthead and and Arten Gill Viaducts, the latter the hardest on the whole line to find a firm footing for. Rumour has it that in an effort to stabilise

Top:
Kirkby Stephen West, on 31 July 1965. On an up freight stabled in the up siding is now preserved 'Jubilee' No 45593 *Kolhapur.* Passing is LMS '5' No 44662 with a Wennington-Glasgow troop special. *The late Derek Cross*

Above:
Milk traffic came from the rail-served plant at Appleby, but this train is misleading for it is the Carlisle-London service, diverted on 1 August 1965 via the Settle & Carlisle. Approaching Ais Gill summit is LMS '5' 4-6-0 No 44675. *The late Derek Cross*

some treacherous clays, bad even by S&C standards a mixture of brushwood and sheepskins was used to try to bind the muck so that solid foundations could be obtained for the arches. Be that as it may, Arten Gill is infinitely the most photo-graphic of all the viaducts in the mountain section . . . once you have climbed up to it. North of Arten Gill, there is Dent station, notorious for snow troubles in winter, then there is another tricky piece of bog under the suitable name of Dodder-ham Moss and so the line dives into Rise Hill Tunnel, the second longest on the line after Blea Moor. These two tunnels are an interesting contrast. Rise Hill is straight, level and reasonably dry. Blea Moor is none of these things. It has a slight bend, and the summit of the climb from Settle is about ¼-mile inside its eastern portal where the 1 in 100 up gives way to 1 in 440 down towards the north. It is wet,

abysmally wet . . . it is full of smells and echoes, and some even say, ghosts. It is a horrible place and I have yet to meet anyone who has a good word to say about it. The station master at Ribblehead who was a keen member of the Home Guard during the war nearly caused an invasion scare by mistaking plumes of steam escaping fom the ventilating shafts on a cold autumn morning for German para-chutists. God knows what the Germans would have made of Blea Moor, especially if one had fallen down a ventilating shaft! On a clear spring day the next 2½ miles to Dent station from the west end of Blea Moor are incomparably the finest of the whole line, with stunning glimpses down Dentdale as the train swings out of cuttings and across viaducts. The bleak blow grass of the high fells gives way to a scenery ever greener as far as the eye can see. There is a similar effect, though not as dramatic, after leaving the north end of Rise Hill Tunnel, with long vistas down Garsdale, the river leading westwards to the River Lune and Morecambe Bay. On this stretch there were once the highest water troughs in the world, sited some ½-mile east of Hawes Junction. Why site water troughs over 1,000ft up in the wilderness? Two reasons: plenty of water and, more significantly, it was the only piece of line that was straight enough and level enough for troughs between Settle and Carlisle. This fact, more than any other, to my mind, sums up just what a unique line this is: no gradient steeper than 1 in 100, but lots of that and curve after curve all of graceful radius, considering the nature of the country.

I have mentioned the anomaly of taking the hard way from Ribblehead to Garsdale and I feel that had it not been for the invention of dynamite, a relatively safe and controllable explosive available by the time the S&C was built, the two great tunnels would have been insuperable obstacles and the Hawes route would have had to be adopted. There is an interesting sidelight on Rise Hill Tunnel before we leave the mountain section for a seam of coal was discovered in the middle of it. This was another S&C anomaly, geologically speak-ing, coal has no business to be there! This has gone into legend in connection with the road from Dent station across the fells to Garsdale. An hundred years ago coal was coal and it drew people to look for it. So small drift mines were opened up on the fells with the result that to this day this road is known as 'the Coal Road' . . . in the vernacular the 'Caw Raw'.

One of the strangest things about the Blea Moor to Ais Gill section is although it is the highest part of the line, once past the summit of the climb from the south inside Blea Moor Tunnel (1,151ft) the line is on easy undulating gradients over the next 10 miles to the ultimate summit at Ais Gill, at 1,169ft. Garsdale is an interesting spot with its bog and drainage to north, west and east all within a mile, truly the watershed of England. Once past the site of Ais Gill's lonely signalbox and loops, the line starts another long 1 in 100

Above:
'Blea Moor has always been my jinx . . .' On 29 April 1967, during the diversion of West Coast trains, a Crewe-Carlisle parcels approaches the signalbox (on the up side) behind 'Britannia' Pacific No 70032 *Tennyson* and LMS '5' No 44674. In the up loop appears to be a diverted West Coast freight train headed by a Brush Type 4 (now Class 47). *The late Derek Cross*

toboggan, hugging the eastern flanks of Wild Boar Fell and at the Birkett Tunnel it passes through the great Pennine Fault where the limestones and millstone grits are left behind, and the warm, red earths of the Eden Valley start. The gradients altereth not with the 1 in 100 descent continuing, with only very short breaks to the first crossing of the infant Eden on the beautiful viaduct set in the trees at Ormside. Set in the trees . . . yes, this is the interesting point, for the last 25 miles such things have been sparse, wind-blown and stunted. The Pennine Fault as seen from above Birkett Tunnel is the most striking geological break I know. Behind you to the south the land is cold, infertile and hard. Suddenly to the north there are trees, green fields and warm, red earth under the plough. As far as Appleby, the villages are still mainly grey stone and the farm houses soundly built against the ravages of the Helm wind, yet the land has a different look, it is mellower.

Appleby might claim to be the only town of any importance on the line, noted for its horse fair. Appleby has an ancient tradition as the market town for the High Fells over the centuries. The first few miles north from Appleby can be considered the dullest part of the S&C with the land relatively flat, though the great hills of the Lake District can be seen away to the west on a clear day. Then to Culgaith with its level crossing, its station that was almost typically Midland in its architecture and its

tunnel, a brief black introduction to the second most impressive section of the whole line, the lower Eden Valley. In all the thousands of words written about the S&C, this is the most neglected and probably the loveliest. I use this last word deliberately for while the heights of Dentdale are dramatic, Edendale wraps you in an aura of sensuality. There is that wonderful view immediately north of the Culgaith Tunnel of the confluence of the rivers Eden and Eamont, the latter leading you straight into the heart of Lakeland, and the charming villages of red sandstone houses nestling by the line: Langwathby, Little Salkeld, Lazonby . . . names that roll off the tongue like a Gregorian Chant. Even the anhydrite quarries at the delightfully named Long Meg had a rustic charm for a commercial operation. For many years I wondered about this name and only on a footplate trip on one of the famous 'Long Meg' trains did I find the reason. By some strange geological freak, this mineral was buried in seams under a big rounded hill surrounded by several smaller rounded hills and the local name for the area was Long Meg (after a local witch) and her daughters. From here to Low House Crossing where the line proceeds towards the industrial outskirts of Carlisle, the scenery is breathtaking. The Eden sparkles through the trees below the line, scintillating with salmon, there are the trees, mostly hardwoods and seen at their best in October rich in autumn colours, and many

graceful if short sandstone viaducts more reminiscent of the Glasgow & South Western than the Midland Railway.

There are the short tunnels with high-sounding names: Baron Wood Nos 1 & 2 where a certain piece of fish attained immortality and, best of all, Cat Clint though what the origin of this was I have never discovered. Then comes Armathwaite station, another delightful sylvan romp to Low House Crossing, and a short climb on to the more open country leading to Carlisle.

Having got to Carlisle, with its connections to Scotland, the Midland Railway skimped neither in frequency of services nor in comfort of their coaches. Though how they did it with the rather puny motive power available when the line was opened is a remarkable achievement, ever at the expense of a great deal of double heading to Ais Gill from the north, and Blea Moor or Hawes Junction from the south. I am not going to go into details of the working and the engines that took part for this has all been covered many times before, as

Two vantage points for a sight of Armathwaite signalbox:

Above:
Derek Cross uses his camera to good effect on the fireman's side of the footplate of 'Jubilee' No 45562 *Alberta*, working the summer Saturday Birmingham-Leeds-Glasgow train on 26 August 1967. This was perilously near to discovering that the engine had run hot as a result of a speedy descent from Ais Gill.

Above right:
Rebuilt Crosti '9F' 2-10-0 No 92025 has been 'put inside' at Armathwaite when heading an up freight on 12 June 1967.
Both: The late Derek Cross

have the smashes, and the S&C had more than its share right up to the end of steam. Two of the earlier ones were the Hawes Junction disaster (though it actually took place at Lunds Crossing) and the Ais Gill smash, the latter about a mile north of that place. They were especially horrifying as the coaching stock was gas-lit and fire added to the terror of the collisions and the stark backdrop of the hills. Apart from man-made accidents, nature has played its part in the tribulations of this high, wild line. A massive slump in a cutting at Denthead closed the line for weeks, a similar slip after a thaw near Long Meg derailed an express. Then there was the snow fiend — winter after winter blocking the line for days, bringing down wires and clogging points and culminating in the terrible winter of 1947 with derailed snowplough engines and the line blocked for weeks. Strange to say, as far as I know no fatal accident has ever occurred up there on account of snow.

Rain and wind also played their part, rain causing the occasional washout luckily spotted in time. I have a vivid recollection of travelling north on the 'Thames-Clyde Express' when we were stopped at Blea Moor signalbox in a storm of monsoonal proportions. The train proceeded under caution through the cutting to the tunnel with the Class 46 diesel locomotive setting up a bow wave across the flooded tracks like a destroyer at speed. The driver told

me at Carlisle that it had been the only time in his life when he had been glad to get into that so-and-so tunnel! Wind benefited the farmers with sheets blown off wagons and sundry other things beside, but it did not benefit me when travelling south one night on what was then the Glasgow-St Pancras sleeper. We repented of our sins for 6hr in the shelter of Blea Moor cutting while officialdom set out in the teeth of the gale to try to find some half dozen cars that had been blown off a train from Luton to Linwood. As one of them had gone over the Ribblehead Viaduct, I doubt if it was of much use to the local farmers . . . the hens would have got out through the cracks. Blea Moor has always been my jinx. The sun went in at the critical moment, I got back to the car to find I had a flat tyre and, on my last visit, an officious signalman (the only one I have ever met on a line where the man in the box was always glad to see you) announced that if I did not make myself scarce pretty quickly he would summon the police from Settle. Knowing the road up Ribblesdale, even a man with a wooden leg could have been having a pint in Dent long before the arm of the law was past Selside!

The Settle & Carlisle was the testing ground for Derby-designed locomotives, just as Shap was for the Crewe breed. Yet neither of the old companies ever really came to terms with these great climbs through the Northern Fells. The LNWR

got fairly near the mark with the 'Claughtons' and the Midland in the days of frequent, but lightweight expresses did well with the Compounds on the 'Long Drag'. But it was not until the Stanier regime was into its stride and Holbeck and Carlisle sheds received allocations of Jubilees and Black 5s that the power position on the S&C settled down. Whatever may have been said or written about the 'Jubilees', there is no doubt that it was on this line that they did their finest work. A footplate trip on 'Jubilee' No 45562 *Alberta* during the last summer

of steam hauled reliefs to the 'Thames-Clyde' express was a revelation as to the sure way that an engine within weeks of withdrawal could storm up to Ribblehead and, unwinded, scamper across the undulations to Ais Gill before running like a hare down to Appleby. Alas, a smell of frying onions during a signal check at Low House Crossing dictated a rather more sober approach to Carlisle . . . the 'Jubilee' had generated a hot middle big end bearing. The work of the Class '5s' was what one came to expect from these engines — a competent job on any type of train. One other class deserves honourable mention in association with the S&C and this was the Hughes/Fowler 'Crab' 2-6-0. Before being largely superseded by the Stanier '8Fs' and the BR Standard '9Fs', these 2-6-0s bore the brunt of the freight traffic and during World War 2 this was very considerable. The last two classes of express engines used over the hill were Stanier's very competent rebuild of the 'Royal Scots' and the Gresley 'A3' Pacifics. I never had the luck to have a ride behind an 'A3' but I am told that they were about equal to a good 'Scot' on the banks and very free running downhill. Hereby hangs a tale. The Holbeck locomotive inspector who accompanied me on my trip with *Alberta* was brought up on that line and in the course of conversation, I mentioned to him that while the 'Scots' went up Blea Moor faster than the 'Jubilees' they never

seemed to make the running going down. 'Too bloody right they didn't, they *rolled*. Hit that curve at Mallerstang a shade too fast and you were still rolling at Appleby.' Enginemen did not like locomotives that rolled and my friend told me that when the first rebuilt 'Scot' that Holbeck received went to Crewe for a major overhaul they found crescents gouged into the frames by the wheels as a result of rolling. I gather the springing was later altered on the 'Rebuilds' and their rolling habits greatly improved. To steam drivers, it was a case of giving a dog a bad name and it stuck. So the 'Scots' were never taken down those long 1 in 100 gradients on the S&C with their sweeping curves as fast as they might have been.

The last recruits to the Settle and Carlisle during the steam era were in some ways the most remarkable of all. They were '9F' 2-10-0s and they are associated for all time in my mind with the Long Meg-Widnes anhydrite trains, and I dare say this is true for many other people as well. But I doubt if they had the shattering experience of a cab trip on a '9F' when we tried to keep diesel express times from Appleby up to Ais Gill, and damned nearly did so. The '9Fs' were ideal engines for this line, strong, sure-footed and with a boiler capable of producing steam for mile after mile on the 1 in 100 climbs with little worries for their crews, apart from rather eccentric injectors.

Oh, I have so many memories of this remarkable line that has become a legend in its lifetime! I have walked nearly every foot of it (tunnels excepted, and nothing but *nothing* would have pursuaded me to walk through Blea Moor) and have absorbed something of its mystique. Its majesty I have tried to describe and illustrate, but you cannot photograph mystique. Is it the Armathwaite Gorge awash in golden autumn colours, or is it Wild Boar Fell suddenly obliterated by a mountain storm, crickets chirping in the blow grass above Shotlock Hill on a summer's afternoon or the Helm wind tearing down Edendale and sucking not only the breath but the very moisture from your body? Possibly it is a combination of these and a great many more factors that arise when man pits his wits against some of the hardest terrain in England. What I do know is that it was a hard line to photograph. The scenery is so vast that you either get the impression of the high, wide-open spaces dwarfing the train, or you get the train looming large and so lose the impact of the scenery. Still, it has been fun to try. Surely, it is a work of British engineering genius so unique that a great deal of thought should be given to its future before any irrevocable decision is made. Surely to goodness, having torn down the Doric Arch at Euston, British Rail cannot do the same for a railway that is even more unique.

A year in the life of the Friends

P. M. Shaw

RIBBLEHEAD VIADUCT, BLEA MOOR.

THE Friends of the Settle-Carlisle Line Association thought 1987 would offer a respite; the Transport Users Consultative Committee procedure was over, and little in the way of activity was envisaged while the Minister decided the fate of the line. How wrong we were! There was not a break for a moment; events came thick and fast to keep our campaign active. It all started in February. . . .

The most important single act of 1987 was the publication in full of British Rail's Financial Case for Closure. BR had previously said that no financial information would be made public, as this was not a requirement under the Transport Act. As the whole of BR's argument revolved around financial considerations, the Friends, Local Authorities, and many others in the campaign were dissatisfied with BR's refusal to supply relevant information. We could not properly fight a case if we did not know the details of the case!

Below:
The regular 'Pennine Limited' Pullman car excursion was worked by the last steam locomotive built by British Railways, '9F' 2-10-0 No 92220 *Evening Star*, on 23 April 1988. The train is passing Ribblehead station, steam working from Carlisle-Hellifield.
D. Stuart Lindsey

Below right:
The 12.42 Carlisle-Leeds at Baron Wood behind Class 47/4 No 47593 *Galloway Princess* on 18 June 1988. *Brian Dobbs*

In December 1986, BR capitulated and issued a three-page press release summarising its case. This was so superficial and open to misinterpretation that it actually made the situation worse. In early 1987, BR released the full Financial Case for Closure and an associated Engineering Report.

The Financial Case is set out as a comparison between the cost of retaining the Settle-Carlisle line, and closing the S&C but instead operating the Leeds-Carlisle service via Carnforth and the West Coast main line.

It is divided into two basic parts for each of the options; the annual operating costs and revenues, and the capital outlays required.

To summarise, BR claims that to retain the S&C would mean a loss of between £464,000 and £964,000 per annum; whereas to close the S&C but operate the Leeds-Carlisle service via Carnforth would result in a reduced loss of between £8,000 and £308,000 annually.

We strongly dispute the figures produced by BR, and have produced our own. BR does not give a breakdown of the revenue figure and we suspect that some important items have been omitted. These include major items such as the revenue from charter trains and contributory revenue (the receipts generated by passengers using the S&C and travelling from other parts of the network), as well as smaller items such as parcels, mails, and other sundries that are difficult to isolate from a general network figure. We also note that no costs are allocated for the maintenance of track and signalling on the proposed route via Carnforth. There must be one, but BR implies that the cost is covered by the existing Leeds-Morecambe services!

Our own figures are:

Revenues (£000s)

Line income	Charters	Diversions	Contributory	Total
1,250	75	150	250	1,725

Costs (£000s)

Amortisation	Interest/ Depreciation	Track renewals	Continuing maintenance	Operating costs	Total
(83)	(215)	(230)	(530)	(799)	(1,857)

This shows a loss of £132,000 in the first year, a significantly lower figure than BR's estimates.

We have then projected the figures over a further nine-year period, to assess changes that BR says will occur. These are mainly a reduction in expenditure on track renewals after five years (when the backlog has been cleared).

By Year Six, the situation changes from an annual loss to an actual profit of £34,000; and by Year 10, to a profit of £94,000.

It would also be fair to assume that, with an expanded marketing strategy, the level of income will rise, but we have not included this.

To summarise our figures, we think there will be an annual loss until the maintenance backlog has been cleared but, after that, the line would run at a profit.

It is appropriate to set all these figures in a wider context. The Settle-Carlisle line is part of British Rail's Provincial Sector, which receives the Public Service Obligation grant from the Government.

Our contention is that the performance of the S&C *within* the Provincial Sector should be the yardstick from which to judge whether the line should close or not.

BR's Annual Report says that, on average, the Provincial Sector only receives 32p in revenue for every £1 of expenditure; yet BR's own figures show that the S&C generates 50-75p in revenue for every £1 of expenditure. Our own calculations indicate that 93p in revenue is received for every £1 of expenditure.

Whether you accept our figures or BR's, both show that the S&C performs much better than the average Provincial Sector service, which leads us to maintain that it should not be closed. It is significant that BR's Financial Case does not put the line into context with the rest of the Sector.

What BR's case seems to revolve around is the second part of the equation, the requirement for capital expenditure.

BR says that to close the line would involve a capital outlay of £381,000. This comprises £181,000 for redundancies and £200,000 to safeguard Ribblehead Viaduct as an Ancient Monument; whereas, to retain the line would require £3.5 million-£5.1 million, consisting of £99,000 in redundancies (for signalmen), £790,000 for the provision of radio signalling and £2.7 million-£4.3 million for repairs to Ribblehead Viaduct.

Again, the Friends of the Settle-Carlisle Line Association have challenged the figure for repairs to Ribblehead Viaduct. We know that the basic figure used by all groups arguing for the retention of the Settle & Carlisle line is one given by the independent engineers, Fairhurst. They said that repairs would cost £2.1 million. BR says that it could not agree to a definite figure because, if put out to tender, different firms would give varying estimates, and BR would like to add a 30% risk factor. This seemed reasonable and we expected to see a range of £2.1 million-£2.7 million in BR's Case; but BR says £2.7 million-£4.3 million, and has declined to explain how the upper limit has been reached.

It is our belief — and we are supported by the independent consultants PEIDA — that the capital requirement is of BR's own making, due to wanton neglect over the past decade. BR's Financial Case admits that 'infrastructure expenditure has been curtailed'. This being so, we do not think that the capital requirement ought to form any part of the decision to keep or to close the line.

Having said that, though, it is obvious that the Secretary of State for Transport *is* including the capital requirement in his decision-making process; so let us examine the size of the requirement.

BR says that between £3.5 million-£5.1 million is needed, whereas our range is of the order of £3.5 million-£4.2 million.

To assess the importance of this kind of sum to BR we must look at other projects on the network. One that immediately springs to mind is the electrification of the East Coast main line. This is budgeted at £306 million, all of which is coming directly from BR, not from Government grants. If BR can afford to spend £306 million on a single project for the ECML, surely £4 million to refurbish the S&C is not beyond the realms of possibility? We are told that ECML electrification is a year ahead of schedule, which must mean cost savings in terms of labour if nothing else; so could

these savings not be transferred to support for the S&C?

During the latter part of 1987 it was announced that the English Heritage Trust have pledged £1 million towards the cost of repairs to Ribblehead.

With our calculations indicating an almost break even revenue position, and £1 million of the Ribblehead repair costs already offset, we think that the Secretary of State has enough ammunition to decide in favour of keeping the line open.

We had meetings with the former Minister for Public Transport, David Mitchell MP, and gave him our financial appraisal.

The Friends were not the only ones to respond to publication of the BR case. Cumbria County Council did too, with an equally strong condemnation.

The County Council's *Case against closure* goes over many of the points we have raised, and its financial analysis shows

Top:
As part of its Golden Jubilee year special programme, 'A4' Pacific No 4468 *Mallard* made a return trip over the S&C on 27 August. Returning to York from Carlisle, the special passes Howe & Co Siding.

Above:
'West Country' Pacific No 34092 *City of Wells* has concluded its main line running for the present. On 22 October 1988, shortly before coming out of traffic, it leaves Blea Moor Tunnel with a Hellifield-Carlisle-Hellifield charter train.
Both: Brian Dobbs

that the line is at, or near to, a break even point. The conclusion of this analysis is that BR would not be better off financially if it succeeds in closing the line.

Once that conclusion has been reached, the decision on the line's future can taken

The beauties of Baron Wood and the River Eden, with autumn tints beginning to show on 18 September 1988. The Sunday 14.20 Leeds-Carlisle with Class 47/4 No 47527.
Peter J. Robinson

on other grounds than financial ones. Points to look at include the social hardship that would be caused to users — the TUCC emphasised that severe hardship would be caused; the effect on local economies — many towns on the route, particularly Carlisle, have realised that an influx of railborne tourists considerably boosts their economy; and the importance of the line as a part of our railway heritage.

The non-financial points are difficult to quantify, but the County Council has tried to undertake a cost/benefit analysis. Its summary indicates that the benefits that would be lost by closure far exceed the costs which could be saved by closure, hence showing that the line should remain open.

There have been several initiatives from the private sector during the past year or so.

The first was a plan to privatise the line; this met with little support as all groups campaigning to save the line want to see it remain as an integral part of the national network.

The second was that BR should give spare land along the lineside to a developer, in return for refurbishing several structures. This idea seemed quite promising at first, but it eventually floundered as much of the land is virtually inaccessible, and there would no doubt be problems with planning permission — especially in the National Parks.

The third private sector plan hopes to provide tourist infrastructure alongside the line that will attract extra passengers, eg restoration of the unique Hoffman lime-kiln at Langcliffe; a major park and ride facility at Hellifield station, noted for its spectacular wrought irownwork; and possibly some smaller visitor centres further north. The details were set out in the Jarvis Report published in the spring of 1988.

While these projects are not directly geared to save the line itself, they would help to provide the sort of attractions that would draw in more people to the area, who would travel by train, and hence increase revenues. Such ventures rely upon the railway as the lynchpin of their operations. This being so, we have given the companies concerned our support and help with information.

Another big step forward for the Friends in 1987 was the introduction of a Local Station Adoption Scheme.

When the Dalesman service was introduced in 1986, all the small stations that reopened to serve it were looking very scruffy — not surprisingly after languishing in limbo for 16 years! BR made it clear that it viewed the new local service as something of an experiment, and was not prepared to put any money into refurbishing the stations while the closure procedure was running. After some discus-

sion with BR's Provincial Sector we secured permission to tidy up the eight unstaffed stations, tend their gardens, and repaint the buildings.

The intention behind the scheme was threefold: to enhance the appearance of the stations and make them look as though they were open; to encourage local communities along the line to take an interest in their stations, with a view to increasing usage by doing so; and to demonstrate that, as well as shouting from

Left:
FoSCLA literature and BR Provincial publicity for 1988.

Below left:
Diversions of West Coast InterCity trains continued through 1988. By midsummer the Class 45 'Peaks' had been withdrawn except for one example retained largely for special traffic purposes. So the combination of Class 45/1 No 45124 (withdrawn early in 1988) and Mk 3 stock on the Saturday 09.45 Euston-Glasgow Central on 2 May 1987 provides a rare sight. The location is Baron Wood. *John S. Whiteley*

Below:
Diesel hauled rail tour — recalling the days when Class 50s headed diverted West Coast trains over the Settle & Carlisle, Network SouthEast liveried Nos 50024 *Vanguard* and 50050 *Fearless* cross Smardale Viaduct with the 'Fellsman' special of 23 April 1988. *D. Stuart Lindsey*

the rooftops, the Friends were prepared to help the line in a practical way.

The stations have now been subject to much elbow grease and present a much more attractive appearance to the travelling public. In some cases, further works have been undertaken after discussion with BR. These include installation of a new wooden shelter on the northbound platform at Kirkby Stephen; complete refurbishment of the northbound waiting room at Garsdale, which had been condemned; and also at Garsdale, creation of a brand new waiting room within the existing building on the southbound platform.

We hope to continue the practical involvement at stations, and were given £500 by Cumbria County Council, who were impressed by what has been achieved so far.

Publicity and promotion was another area that advanced in leaps and bounds during 1987. The Friends have always thought that the key to increasing revenue lay in active promotion of the scenic and engineering aspects of the line. With this in mind we have produced timetable leaflets since 1984. Thanks to sponsorship from the Woolwich Building Society, our 1987 leaflet went up-market to high-quality paper and full-colour illustrations.

By coincidence, 1987 was also the year that the group of local authorities subsidis-

ing the Dalesman service decided to press for better leaflets, too. A publicity group was formed by BR, the Councils, Tourist Boards and the Friends. Each organisation made a financial contribution to Cumbria County Council, who produced a full-colour leaflet for BR. Both our leaflet and the official one used as much artwork in common as possible; and an orderly distribution plan was formulated. The now familiar image of a Class 31 locomotive with six coaches on Arten Gill Viaduct formed the front of the leaflets and matching A4 and Double Crown posters. The publicity material was distributed to stations on BR's London Midland and Eastern Regions, all tourist information centres in the north of England, all railway preservation centres in the UK, and 1,001 smaller outlets.

The publicity group is now a permanent feature and planned the 1988 material, this time produced by BR York.

Continued improvements to services and better marketing are opening up the S&C to an ever wider catchment area with, one hopes, ever improving revenue figures.

The first few months of 1988 were spent assessing the value of the Dalesman local service.

The eight reopened local stations have seen substantial numbers of users, but what is most encouraging is their reason for

travelling. Until the introduction of the Dalesman service, there was a high proportion of 'tourist' users, and only a low proportion of 'needs' users — those going to work, college, hospital, etc. We believed that the reason for this was because the previous services did not allow such journeys to be made. This has been proved by Dalesman; now that a service exists that can be used to get to work and college, the proportion of these users has risen. There are now a respectable number of season ticket holders commuting from the Eden Valley into Carlisle.

We have recently been considering how the commuters are placed within the closure argument. The Transport Act says that any users of any service may object to the proposal. But, as the TUCC public hearings ended before the new service began, the commuters have not had a chance to object. This leaves an important class of regular users stranded without any right to voice their opinions.

Under Section 56/10 of the 1962 Transport Act, the Minister can request an additional TUCC report if he sees a need. We think the new commuters are important enough for the Minister to seek a new report, as an update to the existing one. We have asked him to pursue this, but he says the situation does not warrant a further report.

LMS 'Black Five' No 5407 hammers along, past Howe & Co Siding, with a Carlisle-Hellifield 'Cumbrian Mountain Express' working on 17 September 1988. *Brian Dobbs*

The level of hardship that would be caused has already been classed as severe by the TUCC and now, with commuters to take into account, the increase in hardship that closure would cause must be considerable. It is this increase in hardship that needs to be accounted for by means of an additional TUCC report.

The question of the use of the S&C as a diversionary route remains topical; BR said this would diminish, but it has not done so yet. In the fiscal year 1986-87 there were 217 diversions on 12 days and, for the year 1987-88 so far, there have been 311 diversions on 21 days.

BR has recently abandoned the idea of the Cumbrian Coast line as the alternative diversionary route. This leaves the only other rail route to the West Coast main line as the East Coast main line or the use of buses along the M6 motorway, neither of which is really practical.

With the imminent closure of Wennington signalbox on the Settle Junction to Carnforth line, the practicality of running the proposed Leeds-Carlisle service over this line via Carnforth if the S&C were to close, is being questioned. Will the lengthy section from Settle Junction to Carnforth East Junction be able to cope? It is more than 24 miles between signals!

Looking back, we have had a busy year; and one that has yet again changed the circumstances of the closure proposal. The line is now in good shape as far as revenue is concerned; it is of more importance than ever before to the local communities; and the heritage value has been emphasised by the willingness of the Heritage Trust to make grant aid available. In fact, the longer the discussion goes on, the stronger becomes the case for retention.

	Close Settle-Carlisle and operate via Carnforth £000s	Retain Settle-Carlisle line £000s
Annual Operating Costs and Revenue		
Revenue	400-600	1,000-1,500
Costs:		
Train operation	285	799
Maintenance of track and signalling	—	530
Renewals of track and structures	60	420
Interest and depreciation on rolling stock (average)	143	215
Buses and diversions	120-220	—
Total Costs:	608-708	1,964
Total Profit/(Loss)	(308)-(8)	(964)-(464)